The Tr  d

MW00935811

Hitchcock's

The Birds

ABSOLUTE
CRIME

By Fergus Mason

Absolute Crime Books

www.absolutecrime.com

Table of Contents

About Us

Absolute Crime publishes only the best true crime literature. Our focus is on the crimes that you've probably never heard of, but you are fascinated to read more about. With each engaging and gripping story, we try to let readers relive moments in history that some people have tried to forget.

Remember, our books are not meant for the faint at heart. We don't hold back—if a crime is bloody, we let the words splatter across the page so you can experience the crime in the most horrifying way!

If you enjoy this book, please visit our homepage to see other books we offer; if you have any feedback, we'd love to hear from you!

Introduction

Sir Alfred Hitchcock was one of the greatest figures in 20th century cinema. Responsible for a string of successes running from the 1920s, through a peak in the 50s and early 60s to his last movie, the 1976 *Family Plot*, he directed or produced over 50 titles in a career that shaped the movie industry through his life and still has a massive influence today. He played a huge role in the rise of the British film industry, then crossed the Atlantic and helped Hollywood maintain the top spot. Among his films perhaps a dozen are true classics, covering genres from espionage thrillers to horror. He is probably best known for Psycho, but a close runner up is his terrifying story of a small community under attack by a malevolent flying menace.

The Birds was different from most of Hitchcock's work. Suspense and danger were common themes in his movies, but usually the threat came from people. Part of his talent was in concealing the motives of his characters until they could be exposed as a plot device; until then audiences had to guess much of what was going on, and Hitchcock was a master at inserting misleading clues to throw them off track. No matter how closely you follow the unfolding plot you're almost guaranteed to get a big surprise. In *The Birds*, however, the enemy wasn't a human villain; it was thousands of birds, suddenly attacking for no obvious reason. They had no motivations to conceal, just an insatiable urge to kill. That made them at least as frightening as any of Hitchcock's memorable bad guys.

For admirers of Hitchcock *The Birds* also raises disturbing questions about the director as a person. He was a complex and confusing character in many ways, and perhaps it's not surprising that someone who built a career out of creating suspense and fear on screen might also have had some darker sides to his personal life. In the decades since *The Birds* was made there have been many revelations about Hitchcock's troubled relationship with Tippi Hedren, the obscure model he picked out and turned into a star almost overnight. The real nature of that relationship is deeply controversial, with some calling Hitchcock a sexual predator while others label Hedren a liar and fantasist. The truth, at this point, is probably as hard to work out as one of his intricate plots.

Beyond the details of the story and how it came to be filmed, though, one of the most interesting questions about *The Birds* is why Hitchcock made it in the first place. It took its title from a short story by English author Daphne du Maurier, but beyond the basic idea of people being attacked by birds it didn't take much else from it. The storyline was pure Hitchcock. So where did it come from?

It turns out that his inspiration was a strange and alarming incident that happened just a few miles from his home in California. One night in 1961 thousands of seabirds mysteriously flew onshore and crashed into cars, homes and people along a strip of the coast. Recent research has finally uncovered the real cause of the invasion, but that doesn't take away from the classic that is *The Birds*. As he so often showed Hitchcock was a genius at mixing the true and the fantastic.

Chapter 1: Monterey Bay

The story of *The Birds* is at heart a simple one, and familiar to anyone who's a fan of the horror genre. Particularly from the 1960s through to the early 80s, mass attacks by previously harmless or solitary animals have been a popular plot device for anyone who wants to give their readers or viewers a chill. Sometimes the villains are taken from news stories, like the "killer bee" panic that affected the USA in the 70s and 80s as Africanized honeybees spread north from Brazil through central and then North America.[1] Others play on ancestral dislike of real pests, like rats. Some films have parted company with reality altogether – piranha fish can be dangerous if you fall in the wrong river, but they have never evolved wings and invaded beach resorts.

As you'd expect from the subject matter many novels and movies about animal attacks have been aimed squarely at the low end of the market. There are exceptions though and *The Birds* stands out as one of the high points of the genre. Hitchcock brought all his artistry to bear on it and created some classic moments of suspense.

---

[1] The "killer bees" finally reached the USA in 1985. So far they've killed rather less people than regular bees do.

One question that many people have asked is, where did Hitchcock get the idea? Officially the movie is based on Daphne du Maurier's short novel of the same name, but apart from the central idea of birds attacking people the connection is a loose one. In 2011 a team of environmentalists at Louisiana State University threw some light on the mystery by examining the stomach contents of marine animals caught in 1961. They found that a normally harmless type of marine algae had become toxic, and it affected the brains of seabirds off the coast of California – where the movie was set. For a short time that year residents of Monterey Bay were terrorized by bizarre incidents involving hundreds of sick, insane birds. The truth was a lot less frightening than Hitchcock's film would be, but it was scary enough for the people caught up in it. It also provided a stark example of how small factors can have a serious – and sometimes dangerous – effect on nature.

California has been the most populous state in the USA for over 40 years, but it wasn't always that way. When it joined the union in 1850 it was almost uninhabited, and most of the people who were there had arrived in the last few months to look for gold. Between 1849 and 1852 San Francisco expanded from a tiny settlement of 200 people around a mission station to a city of nearly 40,000. The gold rush faded out around 1855 but people kept heading to California; it was a great place for farming, and increasing trade with the Far East attracted sailors, merchants and dock workers. Ports grew up along the coast and created business for stores, saloons and transport companies. The population kept growing as the coastal towns expanded into thriving cities.

After the Second World War California had another surge in growth. As Americans got wealthier many of them were attracted to the state's weather and its Pacific coast, but not all of them wanted to live in a big city. Small, pleasant coastal towns started to grow into dormitory suburbs, where people could have a good standard of living just a short drive from the cities and their jobs. With automobile ownership expanding rapidly it was ideal. Of course with the population growing so fast there was pressure on the supply of homes, so hundreds of thousands of new houses had to be built. Through the 1940s California's population grew by over 50 percent as three and a half million new arrivals settled in. In the 1950s five million more joined them.[i] During the war and for two decades after it the whole coast of the state was dotted with construction sites, where tens of thousands of workers labored to put up new homes. Every one of those sites had rest rooms for the workers, and most of these discharged into hastily built septic tanks. Some of them had been built too hastily for safety and a constant trickle of raw sewage found its way into the sea.

When we think of sea life the first thing that comes to mind is usually fish, but in fact the most numerous life forms in the ocean are plankton. The most common plankton are algae, tiny, single-celled plantlike organisms that float in the surface water where they can take energy from sunlight. Most of them are microscopic, so they're rarely seen except by scientists, but there can be millions in a single bucket of seawater. Algae are an essential part of the sea's ecosystem – as well as providing food for many larger animals they break down carbon dioxide and produce oxygen, which either dissolves into the water or escapes into the atmosphere. Some of the most beautiful algae, if you have a microscope, are the large group called diatoms. These are encased in glassy cages of silica, a unique feature among algae, and they look spectacular in microscope images. Diatoms are also useful to scientists as a way of measuring water quality – they're very sensitive to pollution.

Some types of pollution kill diatoms, but others can feed them and cause rapid population explosions. When that happens the result is what scientists call an *algal bloom*. Sometimes these happen naturally, but when they occur near the coast it often turns out that pollution was responsible. With many kinds of algae all that happens when they multiply is that marine animals have more to eat, but some species can rapidly suck all the nutrients out of the water and cause major environmental problems. The worst cases, though, occur when the algae are toxic. When that happens it's called a harmful algal bloom, or HAB. There's a more dramatic name for it, too – red tide.

Off the coast of California the most common toxic algae are the family known as *pseudo-Nitzschia*. Not all of these are toxic; some only are when conditions are right. When that happens, though, they produce a chemical called domoic acid. This is a neurotoxin – it attacks the nervous system. It's been linked to many cases of human poisoning because it can build up to dangerous levels in shellfish that feed by filtering plankton from the water; if someone then eats the shellfish they can fall victim to amnesic shellfish poisoning, a nasty condition that causes a range of symptoms including nausea, dizziness, brain damage and memory loss. It can even be fatal; of 107 confirmed cases four victims died.

It's not just shellfish that can collect a dangerous dose of domoic acid by feeding on plankton; some fish can too, including sardines and anchovies. These are small fish that swim in large schools close to the surface, so they're often eaten by seabirds. Anchovies breed in huge numbers off the California coast, and they tend to congregate in and around Monterey Bay; the water is slightly warmer, so their eggs hatch more quickly if they release them there.[ii] The dense shoals of tiny fish attract sea lions, humpback whales, bottlenose dolphins – and birds.

The sooty shearwater is about the size of a gull, with a wingspan of over three feet and distinctive dark brown feathers. They only breed in a few places in the far south – New Zealand, the east coast of Australia, the very tip of South America around Cape Horn and on the Falkland Islands. They can be seen almost anywhere on the world's oceans though because every year they make an amazing migration, flying almost to the edge of the Arctic Circle. Birds from the Falklands have been spotted in the north of Norway, more than 8,700 miles away. In the Pacific they may fly even further; there's evidence that birds from New Zealand travel as much as 46,000 miles every year.[iii] These incredible journeys are made so the shearwaters can stay in summer weather all year round, taking advantage of the better food supplies found in warmer seas. For birds from New Zealand one stop on their long migration is the coast of California.

Shearwaters are well known to fishermen; they often follow fishing boats at sea, feeding off scraps thrown overboard. Fish and squid make up their normal diet and they're very good at finding them. If necessary they can dive more than 200 feet below the surface to snatch prey but they prefer to catch food near the surface. They often follow large fish-eating whales, picking off fish fleeing from the huge animals. Of course small fish feeding close inshore are also a prime target for shearwaters. These fish follow the food sources, and that usually means currents. Ocean currents can move unimaginable amounts of water – often billions of tons a second – and a lot of food gets carried along with it. In the deep ocean currents flow slowly and steadily but close to shore they're often disturbed by the coast or seabed, creating huge eddies where food is trapped. These are ideal feeding grounds for small fish like anchovies, and in turn that attracts shearwaters. Monterey Bay is 22 miles wide and cuts 16 miles into the coastline; tides and the currents flowing up the coast set up an enormous circulation inside it, creating a biological hotspot that attracts just about every link of the food chain.

When many birds migrate they do it in huge flocks. Shearwaters don't – they set out as individuals. There are millions of them though – most estimates put the global population at around 20 million[iv] - and they all migrate at about the same time. That means huge flocks can temporarily form around popular feeding sites, and it's not uncommon to see this happen off the coast of California. Sometimes the flocks are large enough to literally turn the sky dark as they fly overhead.[v] In Monterey Bay it's not uncommon to see over 100,000 of them congregated together at one time.[vi] It's an impressive sight and many bird watchers travel to the California coast every year to watch them, but having so many birds in one place means the results can be horrifying if something goes wrong.

In summer 1961 the shearwaters turned up, as usual, off Monterey Bay in huge numbers. As always they settled above the schools of anchovies and set about eating as many as they could. Anchovies can gather together in numbers reaching hundreds of millions, so even a large flock of shearwaters only makes a small dent in their numbers. This year the anchovies were going to make a much bigger dent in the shearwaters.

Sometime in early August the population of pseudo-Nitzschia algae off the coast of California began to grow explosively as they fed on leaking sewage. Normally most species of pseudo-Nitzschia are only very slightly toxic, but when they come in contact with certain bacteria they begin to produce high levels of domoic acid.[vii] Sewage is infested with bacteria, especially in warm summer weather, and the algae reacted by secreting huge quantities of the toxin. Billions of anchovies along the coast fed on the algae. The fish digested most of the diatom cells and turned it into the nutrients they needed to survive and grow, and excreted the tiny, glassy fragments of the cell bodies. The acid molecules slowly built up in their bodies though. Domoic acid doesn't seem to be harmful to fish – although it's being investigated as a cause of die-offs in sardines[viii] - so it had no noticeable ill effects on the anchovies, but each tiny silver body became a miniature refinery, concentrating the acid to a level far higher than would be found in a bucket of plankton. As the shearwaters gorged themselves on anchovies the poisonous acid started to build up in their bodies as well.

Many algae contain kainic acid, which stimulates the nervous systems of animals that consume it. Most animals have specific receptors in their brains that are activated by kainic acid. Unfortunately the acid molecule is almost exactly the same shape as domoic acid, so the toxin can activate the same receptors. When this happens the slightly different shape of the molecule allows calcium to flood into the brain cells, and it quickly breaks down their internal structure and destroys them. The toxin seems to specialize in memory cells, which store information in the brain.

Shearwaters, like other migratory animals, don't study maps of the routes they will follow as they grow up; they're born with the information hard-wired into their brains. When the time comes for them to migrate environmental triggers, like the temperature or height of the sun, start them on their journey and they follow a series of instinctive commands that take them to where they're supposed to go. A small number of simple instructions can lead to very complex results – this is an area of science that biologists call *emergent behavior* – and this is why shearwaters are some of the most amazing travelers in the animal kingdom. For everything to work they need all the instructions to be available, though, and as they ate the toxic anchovies their brains were beginning to degenerate.

As their instincts became garbled and disappeared the behavior of the shearwaters massed off Monterey Bay began to change. They became disoriented, no longer able to navigate properly. At the same time the acid caused nausea and they started to vomit up anchovies. Large flocks, containing thousands of birds, began to drift towards the shore – where hundreds of new houses had just been built.

Some of the most important instincts for migratory birds are collision avoidance routines. Of course it's vital for any bird that it doesn't fly into things, but it becomes even more important when thousands of them are flying together in a dense flock. Birds aren't heavy but they're fast, and if two or more of them crash into each other they'll probably both be seriously injured. Wing bones are fragile and a collision will probably break them, resulting in a fatal fall to the ground. To avoid that, flocking birds have evolved to be extremely aware of anything in the space around them and automatically maneuver to keep their distance. That's why a huge flock can change direction in seconds – when one individual alters course all the birds around it adjust their own flight path to maintain a safe distance, and in moments the movement spreads through the whole group. Birds do make mistakes – they're prone to flying into large plate glass windows, for example – but in general it's a good system and it almost always works. Now, in Monterey Bay, it was breaking down. On the afternoon of August

17 birds were seen circling over Rio del Mar, a township popular with tourists at the north end of the bay's coastline. That was unusual – normally the shearwaters stayed out over the water – and local liquor store owner Joe Sunseri was puzzled by it. It was about to get a lot more puzzling for a lot more people.

Early in the morning of August 18 a huge flock of shearwaters came ashore at the northern end of Monterey Bay, along a five mile stretch between Pleasure Point and Rio del Mar.[ix] It was a bad night for visibility, with the coast choked by dense fog, and the birds were confused and disoriented. It didn't take long for things to start going wrong.

Around 2 a.m. Gibson Walters was outside his home in Pleasure Point looking around with a flashlight when a large bird skimmed towards him, so low that he had to duck out of its way. Not long after that a sheriff's department patrol car that was cruising in the same area was hit by several birds. Deputy Ed Cunningham had the car's spotlight on at the time, and the confused birds had probably flown down its beam. A teenager nearby was hit by a shearwater as he ran out to investigate the noise.

Around 3 a.m. the flow of birds across Pleasure Point increased. Hundreds of them began to slam into the walls of houses and the noise awakened residents. People rushed outside with flashlights to see what was going on. Most of them quickly retreated as the shearwaters aimed for the beams of light and crashed into them. Above, the birds were hitting the TV aerials and breaking many of them off. Around 4 a.m. a shearwater hit a power line which bounced against its neighbor, shorting them both and blacking out part of the street.

By dawn yards, lawns and streets were littered with hundreds of dead and dying shearwaters. Many had died instantly, their necks snapped when they hit buildings or cars at high speed. Others had broken wings. Many seemed unharmed but couldn't fly – residents saw them hopping along the ground in an attempt to get airborne, only to flop back down onto their bellies. The stricken birds vomited half-digested anchovies and tiny fish skeletons all over the neighborhood. Cats were attracted by the strong smell of fish, then found the place full of easy prey – grounded birds that couldn't escape.

As the sun rose residents tried to do what they could. It was a pitiful scene, and a noisy one. The birds were letting out a variety of noises, some quacking like ducks and others crying like babies. As well as the dead and injured there were groups of unharmed but confused ones, hiding under cars and porches. People cleared away the corpses, and where they could catch the live birds they put them in boxes and carried them back to the shore. Although they'd been helpless on land, many of them seemed to revive when they got back in the water and managed to take flight. It's possible that many of the shearwaters hadn't been affected by the toxic anchovies, but had been forced inland as their flocking instincts led them to keep formation on the ones that were. During the clear up eight people were pecked or bitten by the birds and three of them needed tetanus shots. At the same time Harry Smith, who banded birds to help scientists track their movements, arrived and fitted rings to 65 of the shearwaters that seemed healthy.

The shearwater invasion had been bizarre and frightening while it lasted, and now it left the inhabitants of Monterey Bay with a mystery. What had caused the weird incident and could it happen again? Many people came up with theories to explain it. One of the earliest was that the birds had eaten so many anchovies they couldn't fly properly. That was quickly ruled out by biologists – they'd managed to fly inland, after all. A more likely answer seemed to be the weather. Fog can confuse birds that navigate by the sun or stars, as shearwaters are thought to do. With the lights they plan their course by obscured they often try to substitute other lights. Lighthouses along the coast of California are sometimes struck by hundreds of seabirds in foggy weather and it was quickly noticed that many of the people who'd had the closest encounters with the shearwaters had been carrying flashlights. Ward Russell, a zoologist from the University of California, examined what had happened and concluded that fog and lights were the most likely cause. Meanwhile residents went on with the cleanup and Californians up and down the coast read about the eerie episode in their morning newspapers. One of them was Alfred Hitchcock, who had a home in the Santa Cruz mountains not far away.

Hitchcock had built up a formidable reputation in British cinema in the 1920s and 30s, and by the late 30s he was also hugely popular abroad. Hollywood was already the center of the global movie industry and with his services in demand he moved to California in March 1939. His career reached new heights there, and in 1960 he made perhaps his most famous movie – *Psycho*. That was always going to be a hard act to follow but Hitchcock was determined to do his best. He was always on the lookout for new material he could adapt into a screenplay, and when he heard of the strange shearwater invasion in Monterey Bay it reminded him of a short story he'd read about killer birds.

Chapter 2: The Plot

Daphne du Maurier was born in London in 1907, the second of three daughters of prominent actors Sir Gerald du Maurier and Muriel Beaumont. None of the three girls followed their parents into acting, although all stayed with artistic careers – one became a painter and the other two, including Daphne, writers. Daphne was by far the most successful of the three, turning out a number of well-regarded novels and short stories.

Du Maurier's writing has its critics but it remains popular decades after her death in 1989, and four of her works were filmed, three of them by Alfred Hitchcock. In many ways it was natural that Hitchcock would be drawn to du Maurier's work. Both had a reputation in their fields for creating suspense, so there was a common theme running through their artistic careers.

It's common for artistic people like novelists to form relationships with other artistic people, as du Maurier's actor parents had done. Du Maurier herself made a dramatic exception to this tendency, though. In 1932 she married Frederick Arthur Montague Browning, who had read her novel *The Loving Spirit* the year before and been so impressed with its descriptions of the Cornish coast that he went to look at it himself in his motor yacht. Hearing that the author was recovering from an operation on her appendix he visited her, and after an initial rejection they began a marriage that would result in three children. "Boy" Browning wasn't an author or actor, though. He was a Major in the Grenadier Guards, an elite infantry regiment of the British Army and part of the sovereign's personal bodyguard. When the Second World War broke out in 1939 he was a brigadier in command of a home defense brigade and in 1941 he was promoted to major general and took on his best known job – creating Britain's paratroop force from the brand-new and disorganized 1st

Airborne Division. Browning had a hard war, including a major role in the controversial Operation Market Garden in 1944 which saw most of the 1st Airborne wiped out by SS panzers at Arnhem. It must have affected du Maurier to know that her husband was taking part in some of the war's most dangerous battles, although it later turned out that both of them had affairs during the war. However if the risks were high so were the rewards – Browning was knighted for his achievements, and when he retired from the Army in 1948 he joined the personal staff of Princess Elizabeth (later Queen Elizabeth II). This meant the couple had to keep a home in London, but they also had a residence in Cornwall. Du Maurier's classic 1938 novel *Rebecca* (also filmed by Hitchcock) had been inspired by a huge derelict mansion in Fowey, Cornwall. Du Maurier managed to lease the house, Menabilly, in 1943 and set about restoring it. After the war she and Browning both spent as much time there as they could.

Sometime between Browning retiring from the Army and 1952, du Maurier was out walking near Menabilly when she saw a local farm worker plowing a field.[x] Flocks of seagulls wheeled above him and du Maurier, with her eye for suspense, imagined that the birds might be preparing to attack rather than simply looking for unearthed food in the raw soil.

In the late 1940s and early 50s the optimism generated by the end of the war was fading away, replaced by unease about the new world order. The Cold War was becoming more menacing by the month, with UN troops fighting Soviet-backed communist armies in Korea. Du Maurier tied these new anxieties together with the ominous image of the circling seagulls, and came up with a short work called simply *The Birds*. It was released in 1952 as part of a collection called *The Apple Tree*, which after the success of Hitchcock's movie was renamed *The Birds and Other Stories*.

Du Maurier's novella is told from the point of view of Nat Hocken, a war veteran who supplements his military pension by working part time for a local farmer. An abrupt change to wintry weather seems to bring on strange behavior among birds, with huge flocks of gulls building up around the tideline. The first attack is a gull that taps at Nat's bedroom window, then scratches his hand with a peck. More birds try to break into his children's bedroom. Nat drives them off, but next day he hears that birds are attacking people throughout Britain. Nat boards up his windows and prepares to resist the attacks. A national emergency is declared and the flocks of birds are attacked by warplanes, but the fighters are brought down. This isn't as crazy as it sounds – bird strikes are a common cause of aircraft crashes. Finally Nat discovers that all his neighbors have been killed by the birds. He collects supplies and returns home, but more flocks begin attacking his house. The story ends with him smoking a last cigarette then throwing the empty pack into the fireplace.

The Birds used du Maurier's trademark tricks of suspense to crank up the reader's anxiety. That didn't prevent her from being accused of plagiarism, as she was several times throughout her life. Frank Baker had published a novel, also called *The Birds*, in 1936[xi] and du Maurier had been working for his publisher at the time. That opened up the possibility that she'd read his book and stolen the plot. There were differences though – Baker's work was much longer and set in London, and the birds in it appeared to be supernatural creatures.[xii] Du Maurier added other elements, too. The aggressive behavior of the birds in her novella seemed to be caused by a wintry east wind, and in the emerging symbolism of the Cold War an east wind was a powerful metaphor for the communist enemies to the east. Winter symbolized the freezing weather often associated with Russia, as well as the bitter winter conditions experienced by UN troops fighting the other enemy – China – in the Korean peninsula. That gave her story two layers – a simple but suspenseful horror tale of small animals destroying humanity, and a more subtle parable of western society being overcome by the eastern danger.

Chapter 3: The Movie

It didn't take long for Hitchcock to hear about the shearwater invasion in Monterey Bay, and the idea of it sparked his interest. On August 18, the day of the incident, he phoned the newspaper's office and asked them to mail a copy of the story to his Scotts Valley home. The next day he called them again to tell them he planned to use their article as research material for his next movie.[xiii] By the end of the month the basic outline of *The Birds* was taking shape and a scriptwriter had been hired.

Hitchcock's plan was to take the basic premise of du Maurier's story and move the action to California, bringing in elements of what had actually happened in Monterey Bay. He based the plot around a growing romance between the two lead characters that dominates the early part of the movie but is later overshadowed by the increasing threat from the birds.

The plot begins when Melanie Daniels encounters Mitch Brenner in a pet shop in San Francisco, where he is trying (unsuccessfully) to buy two lovebirds for his sister. Mitch pretends to mistake Melanie for a sales assistant, recognizing her from a court case where one of the practical jokes she loves backfired. Melanie doesn't know this but plays a joke of her own, pretending to sell him a mynah bird.[xiv] Finally he reveals that he knows who she is. At first she is furious, but this turns to amusement as she realizes how he used her own tricks against her. She finds his address from the license plate of his car and buys him a pair of lovebirds, which she secretly delivers to his home. A neighbor tells her that Mitch spends his weekends in a small coastal town called Bodega Bay and she decides to take the birds there instead. She finds Mitch's mother's home and leaves the birds, but as she is leaving a seagull attacks her and she is slightly injured. Mitch sees this happen and talks to her. He invites her for dinner at his mother Lydia's home, although Lydia – who is worried that her chickens aren't eating – doesn't seem keen.

Soon after there are more incidents involving birds. Melanie is staying with local schoolteacher Annie Hayworth (who is also a former lover of Mitch) when a gull flies into the door and is killed. Next day an outdoor birthday party is held for Mitch's young sister Cathy and a small flock of gulls attack as the children play blind man's buff, causing minor injuries to some of them. Later a flock of swifts fly down the chimney into the house.

Mitch's mother finds one of her neighbors dead, apparently killed inside his home by birds. Panicked, she persuades Melanie to collect Cathy from school in case she is attacked on the way home. She waits outside while Annie sings a song with the children, but notices that thousands of crows are gathering around the school. Finally she warns Annie and the two women attempt to lead the children out of the school. The sound of their footsteps provokes an attack; Melanie is separated from the group with Cathy and another child but they manage to shelter in a parked car. As soon as they are safe the birds stop attacking.

Managing to get to a diner in town, Melanie calls her father to tell him about the attacks. Locals are skeptical until a huge flock of mixed birds attack a motorist at the gas station. A dropped cigar ignites a pool of spilled gasoline, causing an explosion and fire and killing one man. One woman in the diner, hysterical, accuses Melanie of bringing on the attacks. Mitch arrives and goes with Melanie to Annie's house to collect Cathy, but they find Annie dead; she has been killed by birds as she pushed Cathy through the door to avoid another attack. Back home they barricade Lydia's house to keep the birds out and fight off repeated attacks. Finally the birds settle and the four of them fall asleep. Melanie is woken by a sound from upstairs and goes to investigate. A group of birds have broken in through the roof and they attack her, injuring her badly. Mitch hears the noise and rescues her but it's obvious she needs medical attention. Carrying her out to the car they find the house surrounded by a sea of waiting birds, which watch them as they get in the vehicle and drive away.

Hitchcock decided to break with movie tradition by not using a conventional background music score for *The Birds*. Instead he alternated between sound effects, carefully selected music incorporated into the plot itself – such as Melanie playing Debussy on the piano – and dramatic silences. An early electric synthesizer, the Trautonium, was used to create many effects including a range of bird cries. Hitchcock also brought in Hollywood composer Bernard Hermann, who had provided music for previous movies including *Psycho*, to coordinate the soundtrack.

Most of Hitchcock's films depended on dialogue, lighting and acting to create suspense, but for *The Birds* it was also necessary to create special effects. Until quite recently this was something directors avoided wherever they could. Computer generated imagery wasn't an option – the combined computing power of the entire world wasn't much more than a single high-end PC now has – and making convincing effects was a slow, complex and expensive process. Even with the best technicians the results were often barely satisfactory. In fact that's one reason Hitchcock's suspense movies have aged so well – modern audiences often laugh at old special effects, but artful tension is ageless. Nevertheless the plot of *The Birds* demanded attacks involving hundreds or thousands of birds, and that meant at least some effects would be needed. Hitchcock turned to one of the leaders of the time – Walt Disney Studios.

In the 1960s the standard way of creating special effects was to combine two scenes – for example, in the British war film 633 Squadron cockpit scenes during an air attack were filmed using static aircraft mockups, then combined with footage of passing scenery. This was usually done by filming the actors and their props against a uniform blue or green background (the background would be selected for maximum color difference from what was being filmed). The background color would then be removed and the remaining image overlaid on the scene footage, then a new composite film was shot of the combined elements. This technique works very well for many purposes, and it's still used for many TV shows – the weather forecaster isn't really pointing at a map; it's just a blank green wall, and the map is superimposed digitally. For complex scenes it's less suitable though. In movies it works to a certain degree but is rarely very convincing. There's usually a colored border around the actors, and sometimes colors from one set of film bleeds into the other one. For Hitchcock's purposes there was another problem with it, too; the technique doesn't work well for rapidly moving objects – like a bird's wing.

Luckily for Hitchcock Walt Disney had an alternative. They'd adopted a technique pioneered by British studios in the late 1950s that used sodium vapor lamps and a beam splitter. With this method the action was filmed against a screen lit with high intensity sodium lamps, which throw yellow light in a very narrow color band rarely found anywhere else. The light beam focused by the camera lens is split, and recorded simultaneously by two reels of film. One is standard movie film and the other is only sensitive to the sodium light. When the two reels are combined it gives a very clear border around the actors, so when this film is added to the background footage there's no border or color bleeding. It allowed the bird scenes to look as realistic as anything that could be achieved without CGI technology. Other scenes were filmed with mechanical birds, and hundreds of live ones were also used.

Of course there was a lot more to making a great movie than music, sounds and special effects. To make the most of the story he'd devised Hitchcock also needed the right acting talent.

Chapter 4: The Actress

Hitchcock operated on two levels; he worked out the big themes of his movies, then paid enormous attention to detail in making sure that crucial scenes were perfectly arranged, lit and influenced by sound. There was a missing level between those that he usually left to others, though – writing the screenplay. For *The Birds* he brought in New York author Evan Hunter.

Salvatore Albert Lombino was born in New York City in 1926. Returning home after serving on a destroyer in the Pacific Theater he took a number of jobs while he worked to establish himself as a writer. In 1952 he changed his name by deed poll to Evan Hunter – a pen name he'd used on some early short stories - as his literary agent had told him any novel he wrote would sell better under that name than under S.A. Lombino. His first novel, *The Blackboard Jungle*, was published in 1954 and was a major critical success.[xv] To boost his earnings he was also writing a lot of crime fiction, and to avoid damaging his reputation for serious novels he adopted more pen names. One of them was the one he'd later become best known under – Ed McBain. Starting with the 1956 *Cop Hater*, Hunter wrote 54 novels in his 87th Precinct series, plus a number of short stories and spinoffs based around the same characters. Several of the books were filmed and Hunter gradually became interested in writing screenplays as well. His first Hollywood job was the 1960 Kirk Douglas drama *Strangers When We Meet*, an adaptation of one of the novels he'd published under his own name. It impressed Hitchcock enough that he hired Hunter to write *The Birds* for him.

When he started the screenplay the lead players Hunter had in mind were Cary Grant as Mitch and Grace Kelly as Melanie. Grant and Kelly had both worked with Hitchcock before, including starring together in the 1955 *To Catch a Thief*. Along with working well with the director they were both big enough names to more or less guarantee the movie's success. This time neither of them was available though. Grant was busy – he was committed to *A Touch of Mink* and *Charade* – and wouldn't have time to take part in one of Hitchcock's notoriously demanding productions. Kelly was also unavailable, but for very different reasons. In 1955 she had married Prince Rainer, ruler of the tiny country of Monaco. Rainer was against her making any more movies, and in fact banned the showing of her earlier roles in Monaco; her marriage effectively ended her career at the age of 26, and when Hitchcock tried to tempt her out of retirement for *Marnie* in 1964 there was a public outcry from her husband's subjects. The director was going to have to look elsewhere for *The*

Birds.

One of Hitchcock's long-term plans was to build his own stable of actors and actresses, tied to him with personal contacts. He had no chance of bringing in the top Hollywood stars – most of them were still tied in to contracts with studios, and the rest were following Cary Grant's lead and managing their own careers. Instead he decided to look for talented newcomers who he could build up with carefully selected roles. *The Birds* gave him a chance to start putting this plan into effect and he decided to choose the leads accordingly.

For the part of Mitch Brennan he chose Rod Taylor, an Australian who had been in Hollywood since 1954. Taylor had played a number of minor roles in TV shows and low budget movies, and had impressed the Hollywood hierarchy; in 1960 he landed his first big part as the Time Traveller in *The Time Machine*. Perhaps Hitchcock saw some similarities to Grant; neither man was American – Grant was English, although he later took US citizenship – but both had mastered the accent and came across as sympathetic characters on screen.

The choice of an actress to play Melanie was more difficult, but finally Hitchcock settled on Tippi Hedren, a model whose only acting experience was in TV commercials. Hitchcock had seen one of these commercials, and in October 1961 he contacted her through her agent. At first Hedren was only told that a Hollywood producer wanted to work with her; when she found out it was the legendary Hitchcock she was overawed enough to sign an exclusive seven year contract.

The first step was to evaluate Hedren's ability to play a role. Hitchcock set up an elaborate and expensive screen test, asking her to play parts from his previous movies. She was nervous, but worked hard to remember her lines and movements.[xvi] The effort paid off; after the screen test Hitchcock took her out to dinner, gave her a gold pin showing three birds and asked her to play the role of Melanie in *The Birds*. Hedren, who had expected a part in the director's weekly TV show *Alfred Hitchcock Presents*, was stunned.

Because of Hedren's inexperience Hitchcock had to coach her in acting as the movie was filmed. Hedren later said she'd learned as much about acting in three years with Hitchcock as she would have in 15 anywhere else, but at the time it was an exhausting experience.[xvii] It took six months to shoot the main scenes and the schedule was so tight that Hedren got one afternoon off a week all through that time. At the time she was a single mother bringing up a five year old daughter, who shared a name with her character – Melanie Griffith, who went on to have a successful acting career of her own. The stress was incredible, but Hedren enjoyed it – at first.

Hedren's most dramatic scene was the climactic bird attack in the upstairs bedroom, and she was worried about it. Hitchcock was firm – the scene had to be done. When Hedren, visibly nervous, asked about Melanie's motivation for going upstairs Hitchcock replied, "Because I tell you to."[xviii] He offered her some reassurance as well – the scene, he said, would be filmed with the mechanical birds that had already been used for other shots. It wasn't. When she walked into the set she found a group of animal handlers waiting with four boxes of live crows, ravens, pigeons and gulls.

It took five days to film the scene and every day Hedren had to endure having birds thrown at her by the gauntleted handlers. Their beaks were held closed with rubber bands to reduce the chance of injuries but even so it was terrifying. Finally a bird's beak slashed her cheek, barely missing one eye. Hedren, exhausted, collapsed and burst into tears. A doctor ordered her to rest for a week. Hitchcock protested, saying he couldn't film without her, but the doctor was adamant. "What are you trying to do, kill her?" he asked.

Chapter 5: Welcoming the Horror

The Birds premiered on March 28, 1963 in New York before opening nationwide, and then internationally. It was a huge success. After production costs of $3.3 million it brought in over $11.4 million at the box office.[xix] It was given a special showing at the prestigious Cannes Film Festival in May and was rated the top foreign film by the Bengal Film Journalists' Association, which is highly regarded because of its influence on the huge Indian market. The BFJA also gave Hitchcock their Director Award for the movie. Hedren was awarded the Golden Globe for new star of the year, which she shared with Ursula Andress (for the first Bond film, *Dr. No*) and Elke Sommer (for spy thriller *The Prize*.) Photoplay magazine gave her their Most Promising Newcomer award.

Hitchcock's attention to special effects had been noted too. The effects had been performed by Ub Iwerks, a cartoonist and technician who had created Mickey Mouse for his friend Walt Disney. His work on The Birds earned him a nomination for an Academy Award, although he was narrowly beaten by the Richard Burton/Elizabeth Taylor epic *Cleopatra*. It was still an impressive performance for Iwerks, as he had been working on a much smaller budget – Cleopatra cost $44 million to produce, but lost $18 million for 20th Century Fox despite having the year's highest takings at the box office.

It's now more than 50 years since *The Birds* was released and it's continued to attract positive reviews despite its dated special effects. Many Hitchcock fans regard it as his last unflawed movie and it's rated highly by the internet movie aggregator Rotten Tomatoes – its rating of "96% fresh" is streets ahead of many newer big-budget Hollywood productions. The American Film Institute rates it as the seventh greatest thriller ever. It's also attracted attention from scholars, with books analyzing every possible interpretation of it right down to a "feminist-vegetarian critical theory."[xx]

The movie has also caused controversy, most of it centered on Hitchcock's relationship with Hedren. There's no doubt that Hitchcock had a controlling personality, and it was widely known at the time that as well as coaching Hedren in acting he was bombarding her with advice about clothes, food and wine. Much of this could be put down to his desire to turn her into a major star, but since his death Hedren has made many allegations about a sexual motive on Hitchcock's part. Although the director was married and Hedren herself was engaged, she claims that all through filming she continuously had to fight off sexual advances from him.[xxi] She could handle the situation during filming of The Birds, she said, but when she again replaced Grace Kelly as the female lead in the 1964 drama *Marnie* Hitchcock's propositions had become too open to ignore.

Hedren's claims have been supported by some –
Rod Taylor said that Hitchcock was extremely
possessive and constantly ordered him not to
touch Hedren after he called "cut," while *Marnie*
co-star Diane Baker condemned the way
Hitchcock treated her and said she'd never seen
Hedren enjoying herself on set. Others have
dissented including Kim Novak, who worked with
Hitchcock on *Vertigo,* and Eva Marie Saint who
was the female lead in *North by Northwest.* Both
of them say they never saw any evidence that
Hitchcock was a sexual predator of the type
described by Hedren. He was definitely
demanding though – Melanie Griffith felt that
during filming of *The Birds* he was taking her
mother away from her. As time passes it will only
get harder to work out the truth behind
Hitchcock's relationship with Hedren. Hedren
herself still admires his work and attended his
funeral in 1980. She does blame him for stifling
her career – they never made another film
together after *Marnie*, but because she was
locked into an exclusive contract with him she

couldn't take on any other roles without his approval. In 1965 he sold the contract to Universal Studios and she went on to a moderately successful career, but never got back to the heights of her first two movies.

As Hollywood does, in October 2007 it paid *The Birds* the ultimate in dubious compliments – a remake was announced. The intention was to stick more closely to du Maurier's novella,[xxii] and Naomi Watts was marked as the female lead. Hedren, who had been contacted in 2005 when the project was first proposed, was highly critical. "Why would you do that?" she asked, "can't we find new stories, new things to do?"[xxiii] It seems that others agreed; after the initial announcement there was no progress for two years. In 2009 director Martin Campbell was replaced by Dennis Iliadis and the project immediately vanished again; four years later nothing more has been heard about it.

Hedren's opinion isn't a rare one – there are plenty of movie fans that resent remakes. Trying to put a new gloss on a classic plot isn't the only way to revisit an old movie, though, and in 2012 the BBC and HBO released a television movie based on Hedren's relationship with Hitchcock. *The Girl* - allegedly the only way Hitchcock would refer to Hedren after *Marnie* - starred Sienna Miller as Hedren, and focused on the director's discovery of Hedren and the filming of *The Birds* and *Marnie*. Hedren assisted with the production and spent a lot of time working with Miller on her portrayal; the two women formed a strong bond during filming, and both seemed to identify with the other.[xxiv] Several scenes from *The Birds* were re-enacted including Hedren's long ordeal with the birds in the bedroom; "I had live birds thrown at me for an hour in this confined space, which in itself was pretty brutal," Miller said, "Tippi endured it for five days." *The Girl* got generally good reviews, although it was criticized by supporters of Hitchcock. Perhaps the most interesting comment was that it would have been a lot better if Hitchcock himself had directed it.[xxv]

Chapter 6: Influences and Reminders

The Birds had a strong and predictable influence on the horror genre for decades after it was released. Anxiety about nuclear war in the 1950s and early 60s showed itself in the "atomic cinema" era, when a staple of monster movies was giant insects or other monsters created by mutating radiation. After *The Birds* the focus switched to mass attacks by smaller animals. Killer ants, spiders and piranhas all had their moment of silver screen glory as dozens of directors tried to replicate the success of Hitchcock's classic. None of them quite made it – movies like the 1978 *Piranha* certainly had their moments, but most relied on special effects and generous splashes of fake blood for their effect. The suspense generated by Hitchcock's direction eluded them.

Novelists weren't immune to the temptation of the genre either. More hordes of small animals crawled out of authors' imagination and threw themselves at screaming victims. In *Feral* by Berton Roueche abandoned cats terrorized a community in Long Island. Edward Levy's *Came A Spider* saw Los Angeles invaded by mutant tarantulas. James Herbert's *Rats* trilogy dealt with a plague of killer rodents swarming through London's underground system. Shaun Hutson went smaller still with *Slugs*. In general the novels did a better job of creating suspense and genuine chills than the movies did – without the limitations of often dubious special effects it was easier to create a slowly rising atmosphere of terror. In *Feral* the cats don't launch their first assault until nearly half way through the book, but the decimation of the local wildlife and the death of their dog are slowly tightening a noose around the young protagonists in their isolated home. The last of Herbert's trilogy, *Domain*, begins with a nuclear attack on London; rats are the least of the survivor's worries – at first…

Of course large monsters made a comeback in 1974 with Peter Benchley's bestselling novel *Jaws*, and Stephen Spielberg's adaptation of it the next year. What set the classic shark movie apart from the 1950s versions – and the many rip-offs released to cash in on its success – was the level of suspense Spielberg generated. If Hitchcock himself had filmed Benchley's book it's hard to imagine he would have done it much differently. Later releases in the Jaws franchise fell into the same trap as the crop of movies that imitated *The Birds*, though – there was no tension. The audience knew there would be a killer shark, they knew it would eat some people, they knew only the police chief would believe it was there and they knew that, finally, it would explode.

Jaws brings us back to the ocean, the source of the strange incident that spurred Hitchcock to make *The Birds*. Leaving fiction behind, have there been any more real-life counterparts to the shearwater invasion? Yes, there have. In September 1991 another outbreak struck – in Monterey Bay. This time the afflicted birds were brown pelicans, and unlike the sooty shearwater – which roams the oceans by the million – this is a species that's hovering on the edge of becoming endangered. When hundreds of them began washing up along the coast, dead or dying, conservationists started to worry. This time they managed to identify the culprit, though. Domoic acid's effects, and the way it builds up in the bodies of anchovies, was unknown in 1961. The crazed shearwaters had been newsworthy but nobody was going to spend a fortune investigating the incident. When over a hundred Canadians got sick in 1987, and three of them died, it was different. The investigation homed in on mussels collected from Prince Edward Island, and tests found that the shellfish were loaded with domoic acid. Mussels feed by filtering algae out of the water; scientists tested the local algae and that was riddled with the acid, too. A new medical condition had been discovered – amnesic shellfish poisoning, named after the memory loss that's a common symptom – and wildlife researchers wondered if it could explain mysterious deaths in marine animals, too. When the pelicans started dying in 1991 their bodies were tested, and it turned out that just like the shearwaters 30 years before they'd been eating contaminated anchovies.[xxvi]

Sadly California didn't have to wait 30 years for it to happen again. Nine months later 400 sea lions died off the coast. Their bodies tested positive for domoic acid. Thousands of birds and mammals died in early 2002. In 2006 pelicans were struck again – witnesses reported seeing the birds flying aimlessly inland, before suddenly diving to the ground and crashing. In 2007 a pelican, suspected to have been suffering from poisoning, smashed through the windshield of a car on a coastal expressway. In 2009 hundreds more pelicans died and over a hundred were rescued after being found sheltering in yards and under cars. A car in Los Angeles was hit by a confused bird; so was a boat in Monterey Bay. Cases of epilepsy and other behavior problems are becoming more common among California sea lions.[xxvii]

In 2011 Sibel Bargu, an ocean environmentalist at Louisiana State University, started to wonder if the recent poisonings might be connected with the 1961 incident that had caught Hitchcock's eye. Bargu was a lifelong Hitchcock fan, who as a child had watched *The Birds* through the living room keyhole after her parents refused to let her see it;[xxviii] she knew about his interest in the shearwater tragedy and was intrigued by the idea of solving the mystery. Marine biologists regularly catch and preserve samples of aquatic life, and she managed to track down specimens from Monterey Bay in 1961. Analyzing their stomach contents she found algae – and three-quarters of the algae carried a toxic dose of domoic acid.

Why are the outbreaks becoming more frequent? It seems that the cause, as it was in 1961, might be pollution. It's also likely that the affected area is growing; recent tests have found rising levels of urea in San Francisco Bay, probably from leaking septic tanks or garden runoff, and urea can spark a red tide.[xxix]

Conclusion

There's no doubt that *The Birds* was one of the highlights of Hitchcock's long career. Even today few horror films come close to the level of tension it builds up, an effect that's even more remarkable when you consider just how little on-screen gore there really is. The stories that have emerged about its filming, and Hitchcock's relationship with Tippi Hedren, also add to the mystique of the director as a flawed and complex genius. Whose version is true? We'll probably never know for sure, and the real story is likely to be somewhere in between in any case. Either way we can be sure that *The Birds* will keep on thrilling and chilling both new and old viewers for many years to come.

And what does it tell us about the real world? The incident that inspired it was caused by a natural phenomenon that's a real threat – both to wildlife and to us. Pollution may be increasing the risk, although in this case it isn't a huge and complex issue like ozone depletion; it's just leaky plumbing. It still shows us how a seemingly minor problem can bring strange and frightening consequences from a direction nobody expects, so if nothing else it's a cautionary tale we should all pay attention to. What are the odds of any of us being attacked by killer birds though? Probably low – bird attacks on humans are rare, and usually it's just a matter of a hungry gull snatching a sandwich from someone's hand. Of course there is one piece of advice we can all take from this strange story – if you're ordering pizza delivery and birds start crashing into your windows, tell them to hold the anchovies.

Bibliography

[i] United States Census Bureau, *State Population Estimates and Demographic Components of Change*

http://www.census.gov/popest/data/state/asrh/1980s/80s_st_totals.html

[ii] The New York Times, Nov 24, 2013, *With Extra Anchovies*
http://www.nytimes.com/2013/11/25/us/with-extra-anchovies-deluxe-whale-watching.html?_r=0

[iii] Proceedings of the National Academy of Sciences, August14, 2002, *Migratory shearwaters integrate oceanic resources across the Pacific Ocean in an endless summer*
https://www.ncbi.nlm.nih.gov/pmc/articles/PMC1568927/

[iv] The IUCN Red List of Threatened Species, *Puffinus griseus*
http://www.iucnredlist.org/details/22698209/0

[v] USGS, Mar 2013, *Sooty Shearwater Migration on Display in Channel Islands National Marine Sanctuary*
http://soundwaves.usgs.gov/2013/04/outreach.html

[vi] trgeybirds.com, *Sooty Shearwater, Puffinus griseus*
http://tgreybirds.com/Pages/SootyShearwatersp.html

[vii] Fisheries Science, May 2009, *Direct contact between pseudo-Nitzschia and bacteria*
http://link.springer.com/article/10.1007%2Fs12562-009-0081-5

[viii] Los Angeles Times, Mar 11, 2011, *Toxic algae may have played role in huge fish die-off*
http://latimesblogs.latimes.com/lanow/2011/03/domoic-acid-poisoning-found-in-dead-fish-at-king-harbor.html

[ix] Santa Cruz Sentinel, Aug 18, 1961, *Thousands of birds floundering in streets*
  http://www.santacruzpl.org/history/articles/183/
[x] Daphne du Maurier
  http://www.dumaurier.org/cgi-bin/favourites/news.pl?search=birds&field=headline&method=exact
[xi] Frank Baker, *Summary Biography*
  http://www.frankbaker.co.uk/biog.htm
[xii] The Independent, Feb 27, 2011, *Invisible Ink: No 66 – Frank Baker*
  http://www.independent.co.uk/arts-entertainment/books/features/invisible-ink-no-66--frank-baker-2226592.html
[xiii] Santa Cruz Sentinel, Aug 18, 1961, *Thousands of birds floundering in streets*
  http://www.santacruzpl.org/history/articles/183/
[xiv] Internet Movie Database, *The Birds*

http://www.imdb.com/title/tt0056869/synopsis?ref_=ttpl_pl_syn
[xv] Ed McBain.com, *Bios etc*
  http://edmcbain.com/eljefe/bio_long.asp
[xvi] Spoto, Donald, *Spellbound by Beauty*, 2009 p. 368
[xvii] HitchcockWiki, *The Making of The Birds*

http://www.hitchcockwiki.com/files/articles/TheMakingOfTheBirds/
[xviii] Inquirer, Aug 11, 2012, *Tippi Hedren reveals real horror of working with Hitchcock*
  http://entertainment.inquirer.net/53591/tippi-hedren-reveals-real-horror-of-working-with-hitchcock
[xix] The Numbers, *The Birds*
  http://www.the-numbers.com/movies/1963/0BRDS.php
[xx] Adams, Carol J., *The Sexual politics of Meat*, Continuum, 1990 pp. 105-106
[xxi] Inquirer, Aug 11, 2012, *Tippi Hedren reveals real horror of*

working with Hitchcock

   http://entertainment.inquirer.net/53591/tippi-hedren-reveals-real-horror-of-working-with-hitchcock

xxii Variety, Oct 18, 2007, *Naomi Watts set for 'Birds' remake*

   http://variety.com/2007/film/news/naomi-watts-set-for-birds-remake-2-1117974282/

xxiii MTV Movies Blog, Oct 16, 2007, *Original Scream Queen Decries 'Birds' Remake As Foul*

   http://moviesblog.mtv.com/2007/10/16/original-scream-queen-decries-birds-remake-as-foul/

xxiv The Observer, Dec 16, 2012, *When Sienna Miller met Tippi Hedren*

   http://www.theguardian.com/film/2012/dec/16/sienna-miller-tippi-hedren-interview

xxv The Guardian, Dec 28, 2012, *If only Alfred Hitchcock himself could have directed The Girl*

   http://www.theguardian.com/film/2012/dec/28/hitchcock-the-girl-tippi-hedren

xxvi International Bird Rescue Research Center, *The deadly spring revisited*

   http://w.bird-rescue.org/pelican_domoic_2006.html

xxvii Science 2.0, Jun 9, 2008, *Toxic Algal Blooms May Cause Seizures In California Sea Lions*

http://www.science20.com/news_releases/toxic_algal_blooms_may_cause_seizures_in_california_sea_lions

xxviii The Daily Mail, Dec 30, 2011, *Alfred Hitchcock's 1963 Thriller 'The Birds' – Mystery unravelled finally*

   http://www.allvoices.com/contributed-news/11195987-alfred-hitchcocks-thriller-the-birds-finally-mystery-unraveled

xxix Celsias, *Acid, Algae and the Case of the Disappearing Pelican*

   http://www.celsias.com/article/acid-algae-and-case-disappearing-pelican/

Made in the USA
Monee, IL
17 June 2020

33755084R00049